David S

About Insides and Outsides?

LAURA SUZUKI & PETER COOK

A PANDA BOOK

General
— PAPERBACKS —
Toronto, Canada

GENERAL PAPERBACKS PANDA EDITION

ISBN 7736-7287-7

TEXT AND ILLUSTRATIONS BY LAURA SUZUKI
AND PETER COOK
EDITED BY DAVID SUZUKI
COVER DESIGN BY BRANT COWIE/ARTPLUS
LIMITED

PRINTED ON RECYCLED PAPER

PRINTED IN U.S.A.

TO OUR SIBLINGS,
TAMIKO AND TROY
& PATTI AND PAM,
FOR GIVING US YEARS OF FIRSTHAND
INSIGHTS INTO "WHAT IS A BRUISE?"--
ALL IN THE NAME OF SCIENCE, OF COURSE.

THANKS TO:

ROGER LAM
DR. TED BOADWAY
      ONTARIO MEDICAL ASSOCIATION
DR. CHRIS CLARK
      BIOACOUSTICS,
      CORNELL UNIVERSITY
DR. DON McEWEN
      SMALL ANIMAL CLINIC
      UNIVERSITY OF GUELPH

DAVID SUZUKI ASKS DID YOU KNOW...

...WHAT OUR BODIES ARE MADE OF?

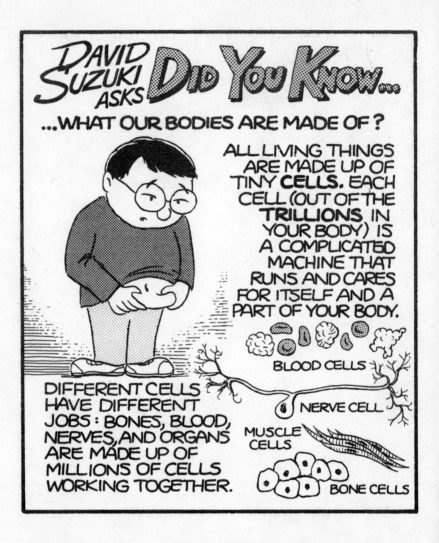

ALL LIVING THINGS ARE MADE UP OF TINY **CELLS.** EACH CELL (OUT OF THE **TRILLIONS** IN YOUR BODY) IS A COMPLICATED MACHINE THAT RUNS AND CARES FOR ITSELF AND A PART OF YOUR BODY.

BLOOD CELLS

NERVE CELL

MUSCLE CELLS

BONE CELLS

DIFFERENT CELLS HAVE DIFFERENT JOBS: BONES, BLOOD, NERVES, AND ORGANS ARE MADE UP OF MILLIONS OF CELLS WORKING TOGETHER.

SOME LIVING THINGS ARE MADE OF JUST A FEW CELLS, LIKE **ALGAE,** OR EVEN ONE, LIKE **YEAST.**

DAVID SUZUKI ASKS DID YOU KNOW...

...WHY YOUR VEINS ARE BLUE?

BEFORE IT PICKS UP **OXYGEN** FROM THE LUNGS, BLOOD IS **BLUE**. **ARTERIES**, WHICH RUN MOSTLY DEEP INSIDE YOUR BODY, TAKE OXYGEN-FILLED **RED** BLOOD TO THE BODY TISSUES.

BLUE BLOOD

OXYGEN

RED BLOOD

YOUR **VEINS**, WHICH CARRY THE BLUE BLOOD BACK TO GET OXYGEN, RUN NEAR THE SURFACE OF YOUR SKIN WHERE YOU CAN SEE THEM.

DAVID ASKS DID YOU KNOW...

...WHY A GIRAFFE'S BLOOD DOESN'T RUSH TO ITS HEAD WHEN IT BENDS DOWN?

INSIDE A GIRAFFE'S NECK VEINS ARE ONE-WAY **VALVES**. WHEN THE GIRAFFE'S HEAD IS UP, THE VALVES LET BLOOD FLOW BACK DOWN NORMALLY.

BUT WHEN IT BENDS DOWN, THE VALVES CLOSE UP.

THEY LET THE BLOOD FLOW UP TO THE HEART BUT NOT BACK DOWN TO THE HEAD.

OUR LEG VEINS HAVE VALVES, TOO. AS YOU WALK, MUSCLES SQUEEZE THE VEINS, MAKING THE VALVES PUMP THE BLOOD UP THE LEG.

DAVID SUZUKI ASKS DID YOU KNOW...

...WHAT A BRUISE IS?

OW! OW! OW! WHEN YOU BUMP YOURSELF, TINY BLOOD VESSELS IN YOUR SKIN BREAK. BLOOD LEAKS OUT AND SPREADS UNDER THE SKIN, MAKING A COLORED SPLOTCH.

AS A BRUISE HEALS, ITS COLOR CHANGES BECAUSE THE BLOOD CELLS BREAK DOWN INTO SMALLER, YELLOWISH PIECES. THESE ARE GRADUALLY TAKEN AWAY, AND THE BRUISE FADES.

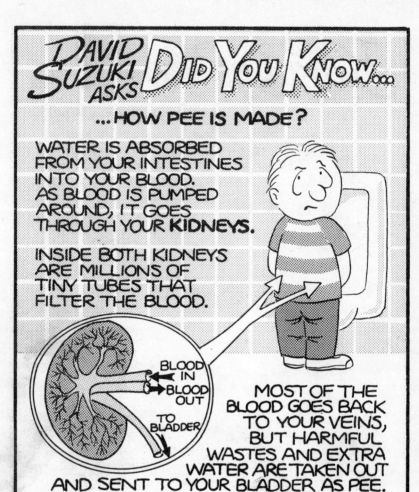

DAVID SUZUKI ASKS DID YOU KNOW...

...HOW A HUMMINGBIRD WAKES UP?

A HUMMINGBIRD SLEEPS IN A FORM OF **HIBERNATION.** ITS HEART RATE DROPS FROM OVER 500 BEATS A MINUTE TO UNDER 10, AND ITS TEMPERATURE FALLS FROM 40°C TO **10°C!**

TO WAKE UP EACH DAY, THE BIRD MUST SIT **SHIVERING** TO RAISE ITS TEMPERATURE TO NORMAL. IF IT IS TOO TIRED TO SHIVER, IT WILL DRIFT BACK TO SLEEP AND DIE.

DAVID SUZUKI ASKS DID YOU KNOW...

...WHAT THE DIFFERENCE IS BETWEEN WARM- AND COLD-BLOODED ANIMALS?

COLD-BLOODED ANIMALS (LIKE REPTILES) CAN'T HEAT THEIR OWN BODIES, SO THEY'RE ABOUT THE SAME TEMPERATURE AS THEIR SURROUNDINGS. THIS SAVES ENERGY.

WARM-BLOODED ANIMALS (BIRDS AND MAMMALS) CAN HEAT THEIR BODIES (SO CAN LIVE IN COLDER CLIMATES). BUT THIS TAKES A LOT OF ENERGY, SO THEY HAVE TO EAT MUCH MORE OFTEN.

DAVID SUZUKI ASKS DID YOU KNOW...

...WHAT A CAMEL'S HUMP IS FOR?

THE HUMP DOES **NOT** HOLD THE CAMEL'S WATER SUPPLY. THE HUMP IS MADE OF **FAT**, WHICH IS USED AS AN ENERGY SUPPLY WHEN THERE'S NO FOOD.

POST NO BILLS

BODY FAT KEEPS HEAT IN. WITH A HUMP, A CAMEL DOESN'T NEED TO STORE FAT OVER ITS WHOLE BODY AS WE DO. THIS KEEPS THE CAMEL COOLER.

UNLIKE CAMELS, PENGUINS KEEP HEAT **IN** SO WELL (WITH A THICK FAT LAYER ALL OVER) THAT SNOW FALLS ON THEM AND DOESN'T MELT.

DAVID SUZUKI ASKS DID YOU KNOW...

...WHAT HAPPENS WHEN WE BREATHE?

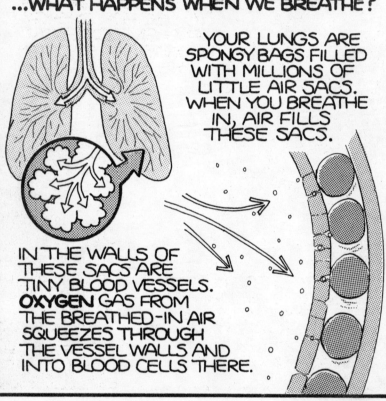

YOUR LUNGS ARE SPONGY BAGS FILLED WITH MILLIONS OF LITTLE AIR SACS. WHEN YOU BREATHE IN, AIR FILLS THESE SACS.

IN THE WALLS OF THESE SACS ARE TINY BLOOD VESSELS. **OXYGEN** GAS FROM THE BREATHED-IN AIR SQUEEZES THROUGH THE VESSEL WALLS AND INTO BLOOD CELLS THERE.

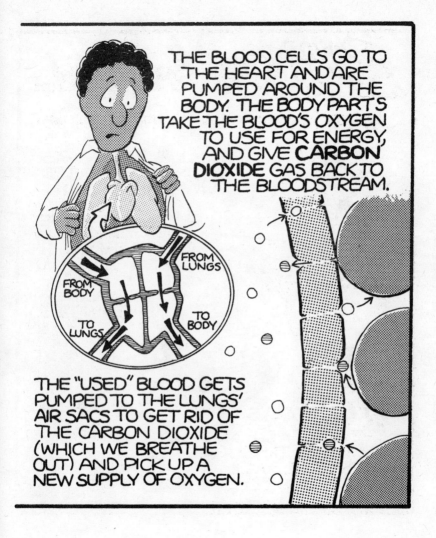

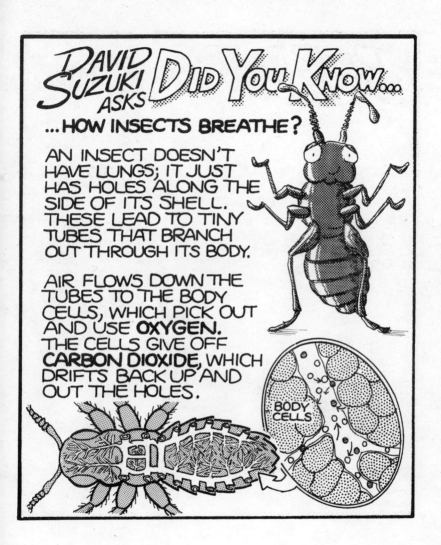

DAVID SUZUKI ASKS DID YOU KNOW...

...HOW INSECTS BREATHE?

AN INSECT DOESN'T HAVE LUNGS; IT JUST HAS HOLES ALONG THE SIDE OF ITS SHELL. THESE LEAD TO TINY TUBES THAT BRANCH OUT THROUGH ITS BODY.

AIR FLOWS DOWN THE TUBES TO THE BODY CELLS, WHICH PICK OUT AND USE **OXYGEN.** THE CELLS GIVE OFF **CARBON DIOXIDE,** WHICH DRIFTS BACK UP AND OUT THE HOLES.

BODY CELLS

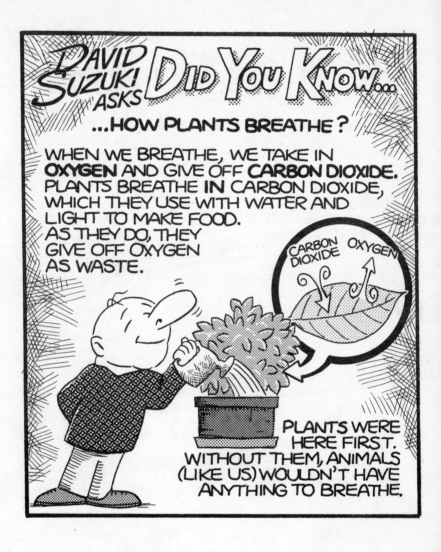

DAVID SUZUKI ASKS DID YOU KNOW...

...WHY YOUR FINGERS AND TOES GET WRINKLY IN THE BATHTUB?

THE THICK TOP LAYER OF SKIN ON YOUR PALMS AND SOLES ABSORBS WATER. IT THEN SWELLS UP AND SPREADS OUT OVER THE DEEPER SKIN LAYERS.

NOT WET

WET

IN SMALL AREAS, LIKE FINGERS AND TOES, THE TOP LAYER HAS NO ROOM TO SPREAD OUT FLAT, SO IT WRINKLES UP.

DAVID SUZUKI ASKS DID YOU KNOW...

...WHY YOU HAVE FINGERPRINTS?

WHEN YOU WERE A BABY INSIDE YOUR MOTHER, YOUR FINGERS AND TOES GREW OUT FROM BUMPY STUBS.

THE GROWING STUBS PUT **STRESS** ON THE SKIN, AND RIDGES FORMED AROUND THE BUMPS FROM THIS STRESS.

FROM LARGE BUMPS, YOU GET SWIRLY RIDGES. WITH MEDIUM ONES YOU GET LOOPS, AND IF THEY'RE SMALL, YOU GET ARCHES.

WHORL

LOOP

ARCH

DAVID SUZUKI ASKS DID YOU KNOW...

...WHAT THE POWDER FROM A BUTTERFLY'S WING IS?

THE POWDER IS MILLIONS OF TINY COLORED **SCALES**, LAYERED LIKE SHINGLES ON THE BUTTERFLY'S WINGS. THE SCALES HELP TO KEEP THE INSECT WARM; WITHOUT THEM, THE WING WOULD BE SEE-THROUGH, LIKE A FLY'S.

BUT IF THE BUTTERFLY LOSES TOO MANY SCALES, IT WILL BE UNBALANCED AND NOT BE ABLE TO FLY.

DAVID SUZUKI ASKS DID YOU KNOW...

...WHY SHARK SKIN IS SO ROUGH?

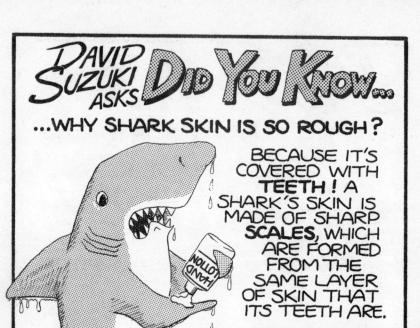

BECAUSE IT'S COVERED WITH **TEETH**! A SHARK'S SKIN IS MADE OF SHARP **SCALES**, WHICH ARE FORMED FROM THE SAME LAYER OF SKIN THAT ITS TEETH ARE.

THE SCALES ARE COVERED WITH HARD STUFF CALLED **DENTINE**, WHICH IS WHAT'S INSIDE TEETH. THEY ALSO HAVE NERVES AND BLOOD VESSELS, LIKE TEETH.

...WHY GERBILS CHEW SO MUCH?

GERBILS--AND OTHER RODENTS LIKE BEAVERS, GUINEA PIGS, RATS, AND MICE-- HAVE FRONT TEETH THAT ARE ALWAYS GROWING.

THEY'VE GOT TO CONSTANTLY GNAW THINGS TO WEAR DOWN THEIR TEETH.

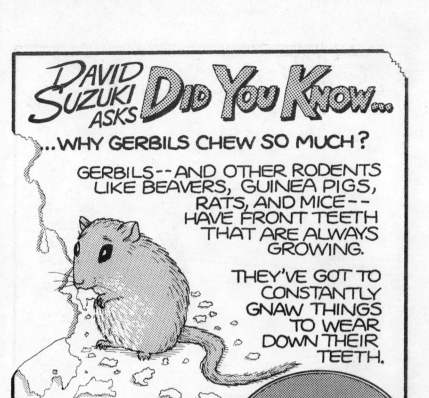

IF THE TEETH WEREN'T WORN DOWN, THEY WOULD GROW UNTIL THE GERBIL COULDN'T CLOSE ITS MOUTH TO EAT.

DAVID SUZUKI ASKS DID YOU KNOW...

...THAT YOUR BONES HAVE HOLES?

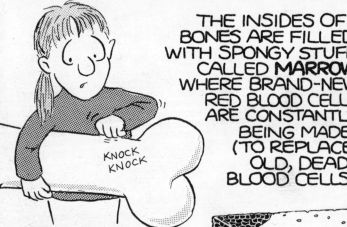

THE INSIDES OF BONES ARE FILLED WITH SPONGY STUFF CALLED **MARROW**, WHERE BRAND-NEW RED BLOOD CELLS ARE CONSTANTLY BEING MADE (TO REPLACE OLD, DEAD BLOOD CELLS).

KNOCK KNOCK

BONES ARE FILLED WITH TINY HOLES SO THAT THE NEW BLOOD CELLS CAN GET OUT, AND SO THE BONE CELLS CAN GET NUTRIENTS, TOO.

DAVID SUZUKI ASKS DID YOU KNOW...

...HOW A WOODPECKER EATS?

AFTER DRILLING A HOLE IN A TREE WITH ITS BEAK, A WOODPECKER SEARCHES INSIDE THE HOLE WITH ITS LONG, STICKY TONGUE TO FIND INSECTS TO EAT.

ITS TONGUE IS **SPIKED** TO SPEAR BUGS, AND IS ATTACHED TO A STRETCHY **BONE** THAT IS SO LONG THAT IT CURLS OVER THE TOP OF ITS SKULL AND INTO ITS RIGHT NOSTRIL.

BONE   TONGUE

DAVID SUZUKI ASKS DID YOU KNOW...

...HOW FLOUNDERS GROW UP?

FLOUNDERS SWIM FLAT ON THE OCEAN'S BOTTOM, WHERE THEIR FOOD IS. BUT WHEN THEY ARE BABIES, THEY LOOK AND SWIM LIKE NORMAL FISH.

AS THEY GROW UP, THEY START TO TILT TO ONE SIDE UNTIL THEY LIE FLAT. AS THEY DO, ONE EYE **MOVES**, GROWING OVER THE TOP OF THE HEAD UNTIL BOTH EYES ARE ON THE NEW TOP SIDE.

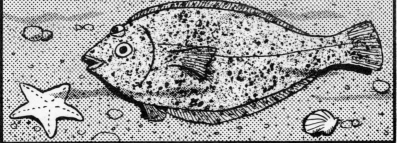

DAVID SUZUKI ASKS DID YOU KNOW...

...WHAT BEING "DOUBLE-JOINTED" MEANS?

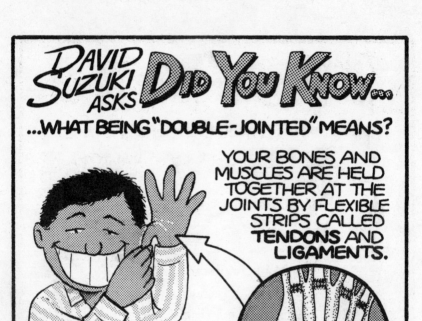

YOUR BONES AND MUSCLES ARE HELD TOGETHER AT THE JOINTS BY FLEXIBLE STRIPS CALLED **TENDONS** AND **LIGAMENTS**.

IN MOST PEOPLE, THESE STRIPS HOLD EVERYTHING TOGETHER PRETTY TIGHTLY.

BUT "DOUBLE-JOINTED" PEOPLE HAVE SOME LOOSE TENDONS AND LIGAMENTS, SO THEY CAN BEND THINGS IN INTERESTING WAYS.

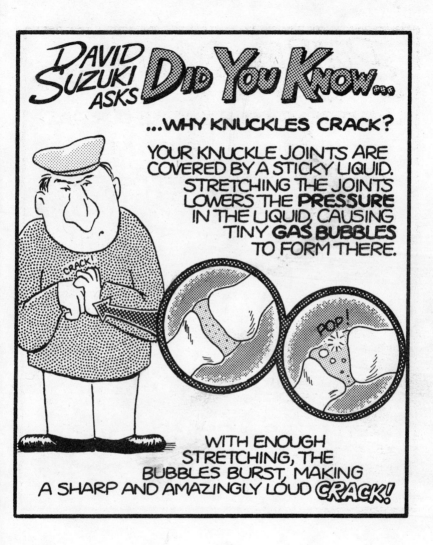

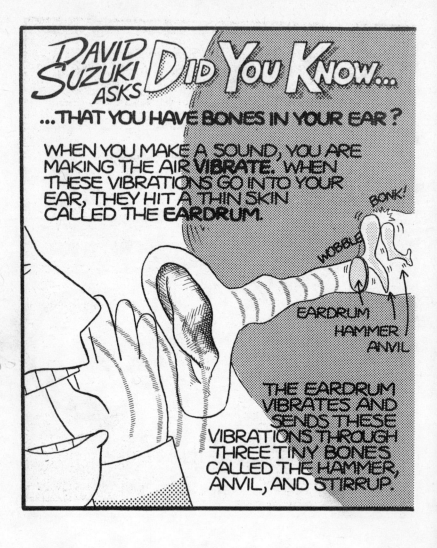

DAVID SUZUKI ASKS DID YOU KNOW...

...THAT YOU HAVE BONES IN YOUR EAR?

WHEN YOU MAKE A SOUND, YOU ARE MAKING THE AIR **VIBRATE**. WHEN THESE VIBRATIONS GO INTO YOUR EAR, THEY HIT A THIN SKIN CALLED THE **EARDRUM**.

BONK!

WOBBLE

EARDRUM

HAMMER

ANVIL

THE EARDRUM VIBRATES AND SENDS THESE VIBRATIONS THROUGH THREE TINY BONES CALLED THE HAMMER, ANVIL, AND STIRRUP.

DAVID SUZUKI ASKS DID YOU KNOW...

...IF BUGS HAVE EARS?

ONLY A FEW DO. THEIR EARS ARE THIN PATCHES OF SKIN ON THEIR BODY OR LEGS THAT **VIBRATE** WHEN SOUND HITS THEM (JUST LIKE THE SKIN IN YOUR EARDRUMS).

BUT INSECTS WITHOUT EARS CAN HEAR, TOO. THEY HAVE SPECIAL HAIRS ON THEIR BODIES OR ANTENNAE THAT VIBRATE WHEN SOUND HITS THEM.

BLUE AND **FIN** WHALES
CAN HEAR FOR HUNDREDS
OF KILOMETERS. BUT
WITHOUT SHIPS, THEY
COULD HEAR TWICE AS FAR.

DAVID SUZUKI ASKS DID YOU KNOW...

...WHY YOU GET DIZZY?

YOU KEEP YOUR BALANCE BY USING INFORMATION FROM YOUR EYES AND JELLY-FILLED **TUBES** INSIDE YOUR EARS.

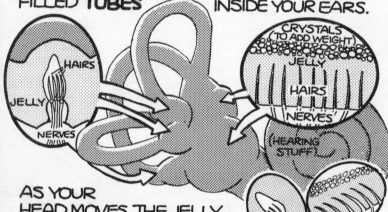

HAIRS

JELLY

NERVES

CRYSTALS (TO ADD WEIGHT)

JELLY

HAIRS

NERVES

(HEARING STUFF)

AS YOUR HEAD MOVES, THE JELLY MOVES. THIS BENDS HAIR-LIKE **NERVES** STUCK IN THE JELLY, WHICH SEND SIGNALS TO YOUR BRAIN. EACH TUBE SENSES A DIFFERENT DIRECTION OF MOVEMENT BEST.

WHEN YOU SPIN, THE JELLY LEANS TO ONE SIDE IN SOME OF THE TUBES. IF YOU CHANGE SPEED, OR WOBBLE, OR STOP, IT TAKES A MOMENT FOR THE JELLY TO CHANGE ITS MOVEMENT.

BECAUSE OF THIS WOBBLING, THE SIGNALS FROM THE TUBES DON'T ALWAYS MATCH WHAT YOUR EYES ARE SEEING.

PRESIDE

YOUR BRAIN GETS CONFUSED BY THIS, AND YOU GET DIZZY.

YOU GET **CARSICK** FOR THE SAME REASONS: YOUR EYES DON'T AGREE WITH THE SIGNALS FROM YOUR EARS' SLOSHING JELLY.

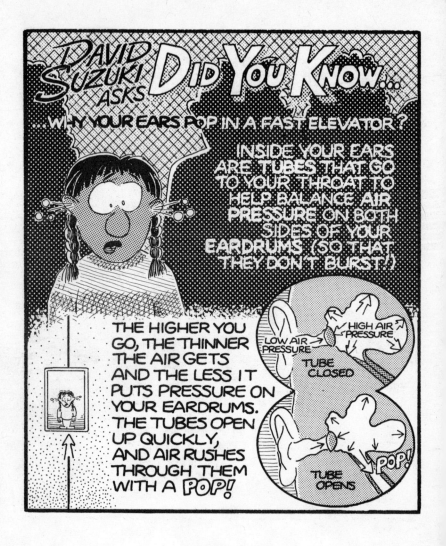

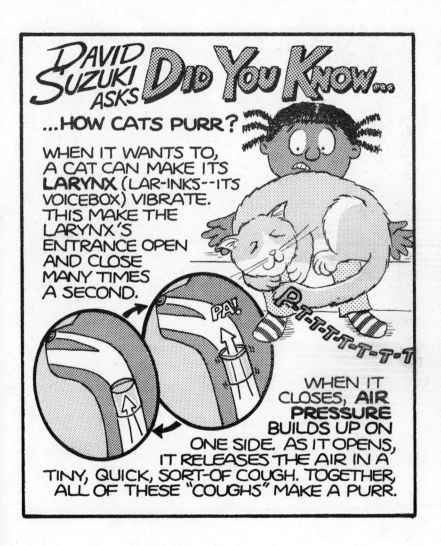

DAVID SUZUKI ASKS DID YOU KNOW...

...HOW CATS PURR?

WHEN IT WANTS TO, A CAT CAN MAKE ITS **LARYNX** (LAR-INKS--ITS VOICEBOX) VIBRATE. THIS MAKE THE LARYNX'S ENTRANCE OPEN AND CLOSE MANY TIMES A SECOND.

PA!

P-T-T-T-T-T-T-T

WHEN IT CLOSES, **AIR PRESSURE** BUILDS UP ON ONE SIDE. AS IT OPENS, IT RELEASES THE AIR IN A TINY, QUICK, SORT-OF COUGH. TOGETHER, ALL OF THESE "COUGHS" MAKE A PURR.

DAVID SUZUKI ASKS **DID YOU KNOW...**

...WHY HEAD HAIR GROWS LONG, BUT BODY HAIR DOESN'T?

A HAIR GOES THROUGH TWO STAGES IN ITS LIFE : A **GROWING** ONE, WHEN THE HAIR GETS LONGER, AND THEN A **RESTING**, NON-GROWING ONE, THEN IT FALLS OUT.

HEAD HAIR HAS A LONG GROWING STAGE (TWO TO EIGHT YEARS) AND A SHORT RESTING STAGE (A FEW MONTHS). BODY HAIR SPENDS ALMOST ALL OF ITS TIME RESTING, AND DROPS OUT SOONER.

DAVID SUZUKI ASKS DID YOU KNOW...

...WHY SOME PEOPLE'S HAIR IS CURLY?

CURLY HAIR CAN BE MADE TWO DIFFERENT WAYS:

HAIR IS MADE OF DEAD CELLS, SOME LARGE, SOME SMALL. IF THE SMALLER CELLS FORM MORE ON ONE SIDE OF THE HAIR, THE HAIR WILL CURVE TOWARD THAT SIDE.

ALSO, IF A FOLLICLE (HAIR PORE) IS CURVED, THE HAIR THAT GROWS FROM IT WILL BE CURVED.

DAVID SUZUKI ASKS DID YOU KNOW...

...WHY CATS HAVE WHISKERS?

WHISKERS ARE LONG, STIFF HAIRS WITH **ROOTS** THAT ARE CONNECTED TO **NERVES.**

THE HAIRS ACT LIKE **FEELERS,** HELPING THE CAT TOUCH AND SENSE THINGS.

WHEN ITS WHISKERS ARE TOUCHED THE CAT'S EYES INSTANTLY **BLINK.** THIS HELPS PROTECT ITS EYES FROM OBJECTS THAT MIGHT BE DANGEROUS.

DAVID SUZUKI ASKS **DID YOU KNOW...**

...THAT YOU'RE NEVER REALLY ALONE?

ALL SORTS OF BACTERIA LIVE ON AND INSIDE YOUR BODY.

ALSO, ALMOST ALL PEOPLE -- EXCEPT FOR REALLY YOUNG KIDS -- HAVE TINY **MITES** ON THEIR FACES.

HAIR

OIL GLAND

MITE

THESE MITES LIVE AND EAT IN THE **OIL GLANDS** INSIDE YOUR HAIR PORES. YOUR FACE CAN HAVE THOUSANDS, BUT YOU CAN'T SEE THEM OR BE HURT BY THEM.

SKIN **GLANDS** ARE LITTLE FACTORIES THAT PUMP OUT OIL OR SWEAT.

...WHAT THE DIFFERENCE IS BETWEEN VIRUSES AND BACTERIA?

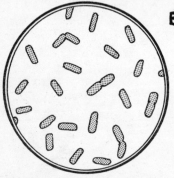

BACTERIA ARE TINY LIVING THINGS. NO ONE IS SURE WHETHER THEY SHOULD BE CALLED PLANTS OR ANIMALS. THEY LIVE EVERYWHERE AND MULTIPLY BY SPLITTING IN HALF.

SOME BACTERIA ARE DISEASE GERMS, BUT OTHERS ARE HELPFUL. BACTERIA IN SOIL BREAK DOWN DEAD STUFF; OTHER KINDS OF BACTERIA TURN MILK INTO CHEESE OR YOGURT.

VIRUSES ARE **MUCH** SMALLER THAN BACTERIA. THEY ARE ON THE BORDERLINE OF LIVING AND NON-LIVING THINGS. ALL THEY CONTAIN IS A BIT OF PROTEIN AND SOME INSTRUCTIONS FOR MAKING COPIES OF OF THEMSELVES.

INSTRUCTIONS

PROTEIN

VIRUSES CAN MULTIPLY ONLY INSIDE AN ANIMAL'S OR PLANT'S CELLS. A VIRUS TELLS A CELL TO DO NOTHING BUT MAKE MORE VIRUSES. THE NEW VIRUSES SPREAD TO OTHER CELLS, CAUSING DISEASE.

RIP!

COLDS ARE CAUSED BY VIRUSES, SO ANTI-BACTERIA MEDICINES (LIKE **PENICILLIN**) DON'T WORK AGAINST THEM.

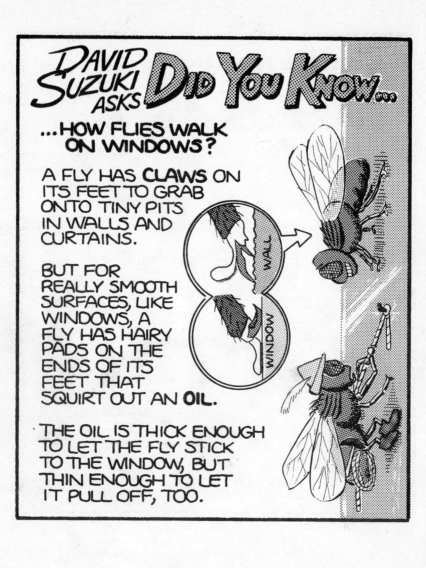

DAVID SUZUKI ASKS DID YOU KNOW...

...HOW FLIES WALK ON WINDOWS?

A FLY HAS **CLAWS** ON ITS FEET TO GRAB ONTO TINY PITS IN WALLS AND CURTAINS.

BUT FOR REALLY SMOOTH SURFACES, LIKE WINDOWS, A FLY HAS HAIRY PADS ON THE ENDS OF ITS FEET THAT SQUIRT OUT AN **OIL**.

THE OIL IS THICK ENOUGH TO LET THE FLY STICK TO THE WINDOW, BUT THIN ENOUGH TO LET IT PULL OFF, TOO.

WALL

WINDOW

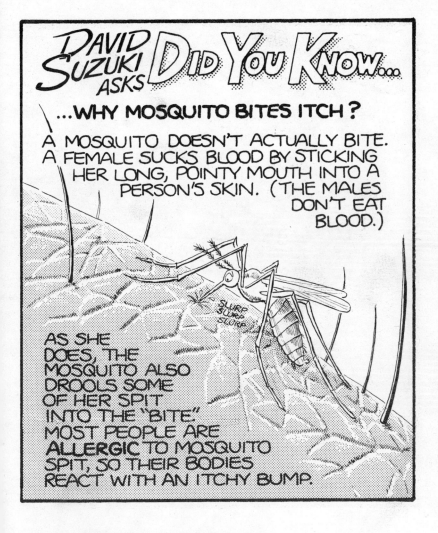

DAVID SUZUKI ASKS DID YOU KNOW...

...WHY MOSQUITO BITES ITCH?

A MOSQUITO DOESN'T ACTUALLY BITE. A FEMALE SUCKS BLOOD BY STICKING HER LONG, POINTY MOUTH INTO A PERSON'S SKIN. (THE MALES DON'T EAT BLOOD.)

SLURP SLURP SLURP

AS SHE DOES, THE MOSQUITO ALSO DROOLS SOME OF HER SPIT INTO THE "BITE." MOST PEOPLE ARE **ALLERGIC** TO MOSQUITO SPIT, SO THEIR BODIES REACT WITH AN ITCHY BUMP.

THE FEMALE NEEDS BLOOD TO BE ABLE TO MAKE EGGS, BUT SHE CAN LIVE ON WHAT THE MALES EAT-- NECTAR AND FRUIT JUICES.

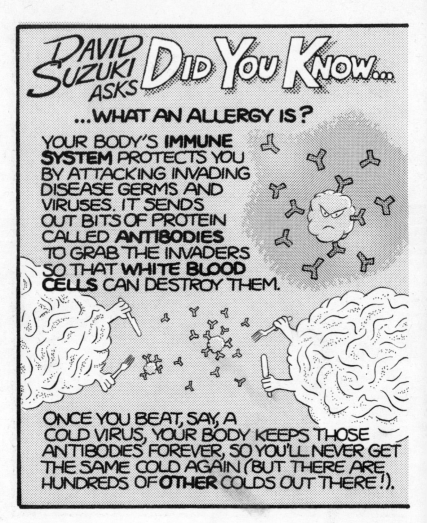

DAVID SUZUKI ASKS DID YOU KNOW...

...WHAT AN ALLERGY IS?

YOUR BODY'S **IMMUNE SYSTEM** PROTECTS YOU BY ATTACKING INVADING DISEASE GERMS AND VIRUSES. IT SENDS OUT BITS OF PROTEIN CALLED **ANTIBODIES** TO GRAB THE INVADERS SO THAT **WHITE BLOOD CELLS** CAN DESTROY THEM.

ONCE YOU BEAT, SAY, A COLD VIRUS, YOUR BODY KEEPS THOSE ANTIBODIES FOREVER, SO YOU'LL NEVER GET THE SAME COLD AGAIN (BUT THERE ARE HUNDREDS OF **OTHER** COLDS OUT THERE!).

BUT SOMETIMES THE IMMUNE SYSTEM PROTECTS YOU TOO MUCH. SOME PEOPLE HAVE ANTIBODIES THAT SEE HARMLESS THINGS, LIKE DUST AND POLLEN, AS ENEMIES.

SNORT

SNIFF

THE ANTIBODIES FIGHT THESE HARMLESS THINGS SO MUCH THAT THEY MAKE THE BODY CELLS SEND OUT A CHEMICAL CALLED **HISTAMINE** (HIS-TUH-MEEN).

HISTAMINE CAUSES ALL OF THE YUKKY, DRIPPY, AND ITCHY ALLERGY THINGS TO HAPPEN--SNIFF.

...WHY YOU MAY GET HEADACHES WHEN YOU EAT ICE CREAM?

AT THE BACK OF THE THROAT ARE **ARTERIES** AND **NERVES** THAT GO TO THE FRONT OF YOUR HEAD. WHEN YOU QUICKLY SWALLOW ICE CREAM, YOU **CHILL** THE ARTERIES.

ICE CREAM
CHOCO-NUT
MARSHMALLO
YUM-YUM

THIS CHILLING BUGS THE NERVES, WHICH THEN SEND **PAIN SIGNALS** TO YOUR FOREHEAD, GIVING YOU A SHORT, SPLITTING HEADACHE.

DAVID SUZUKI ASKS DID YOU KNOW...

...WHY SOME PEOPLE FAINT WHEN **THEY GET SCARED?**

YOUR BRAIN AUTOMATICALLY CONTROLS WHAT YOUR BODY DOES, USING TWO INSIDE **SYSTEMS** THAT WORK IN **BALANCE.**

ONE SYSTEM GETS YOUR BODY READY FOR **FIGHTING** OR **RUNNING AWAY.** IT MAKES YOU BREATHE FASTER AND YOUR HEART PUMP QUICKER.

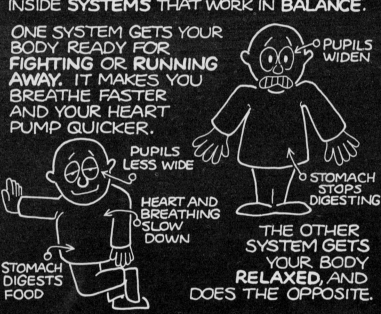

PUPILS WIDEN

PUPILS LESS WIDE

HEART AND BREATHING SLOW DOWN

STOMACH STOPS DIGESTING

STOMACH DIGESTS FOOD

THE OTHER SYSTEM GETS YOUR BODY **RELAXED,** AND DOES THE OPPOSITE.

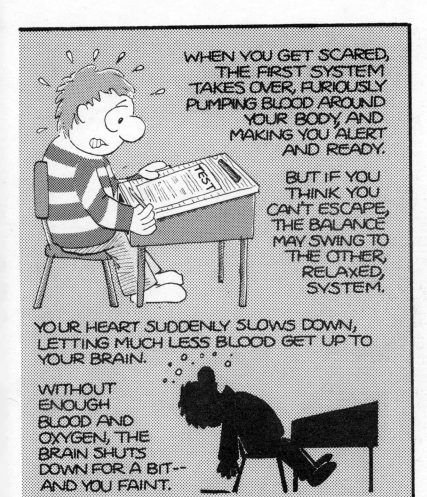

WHEN YOU GET SCARED, THE FIRST SYSTEM TAKES OVER, FURIOUSLY PUMPING BLOOD AROUND YOUR BODY, AND MAKING YOU ALERT AND READY.

BUT IF YOU THINK YOU CAN'T ESCAPE, THE BALANCE MAY SWING TO THE OTHER, RELAXED, SYSTEM.

YOUR HEART SUDDENLY SLOWS DOWN, LETTING MUCH LESS BLOOD GET UP TO YOUR BRAIN.

WITHOUT ENOUGH BLOOD AND OXYGEN, THE BRAIN SHUTS DOWN FOR A BIT-- AND YOU FAINT.

WHEN YOU'RE NERVOUS, AND YOUR STOMACH STOPS DIGESTING, THE SUDDEN CHANGE FEELS LIKE "BUTTERFLIES" IN YOUR STOMACH.

DAVID SUZUKI ASKS DID YOU KNOW...

...IF PORCUPINES THROW THEIR QUILLS?

WHEN PORCUPINES SEE AN ENEMY, THEIR NERVES CAUSE AN **EMERGENCY REACTION**: MUSCLES IN THEIR SKIN SUDDENLY RAISE THEIR HAIR AND QUILLS (THE SAME MUSCLES THAT GIVE PEOPLE GOOSEBUMPS).

SOME QUILLS ARE LOOSE AND CAN FLY OUT WHEN THIS HAPPENS, BUT THEY'RE NOT REALLY AIMED OR THROWN BY THE PORCUPINE.

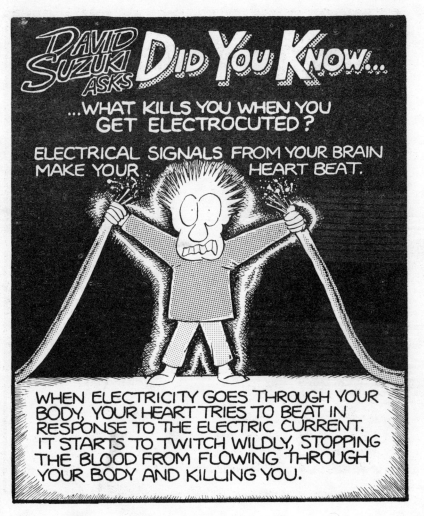

DAVID SUZUKI ASKS DID YOU KNOW...

...WHAT KILLS YOU WHEN YOU GET ELECTROCUTED?

ELECTRICAL SIGNALS FROM YOUR BRAIN MAKE YOUR HEART BEAT.

WHEN ELECTRICITY GOES THROUGH YOUR BODY, YOUR HEART TRIES TO BEAT IN RESPONSE TO THE ELECTRIC CURRENT. IT STARTS TO TWITCH WILDLY, STOPPING THE BLOOD FROM FLOWING THROUGH YOUR BODY AND KILLING YOU.

NERVES FROM YOUR BRAIN ALSO CONTROL YOUR BREATHING. WHEN THESE GET BOTHERED (SAY, BY SWALLOWING), YOU GET HICCUPS.

HIC!

DAVID SUZUKI ASKS DID YOU KNOW...

...WHY YOUR DOCTOR TAPS YOUR KNEE?

MUSCLES WORK BY **CONTRACTING** (GETTING SHORTER). THE DOCTOR'S TAP STRETCHES THE KNEE MUSCLE A BIT. THIS SENDS SIGNALS THROUGH A NERVE TO YOUR **SPINAL CORD.**

SPINAL CORD

MUSCLE

NERVE

A NERVE **FROM** THE SPINAL CORD TELLS THE STRETCHED MUSCLE TO CONTRACT. IT DOES, SO YOUR LEG KICKS UP. THIS MEANS THAT YOUR NERVES ARE OKAY.

DAVID SUZUKI ASKS DID YOU KNOW...

...HOW FLEAS JUMP SO HIGH?

FLEAS CAN JUMP UP TO **150 TIMES** THEIR OWN LENGTH (THAT'S LIKE YOU JUMPING OVER THREE HOCKEY RINKS END TO END!).

TO JUMP, THE FLEA PUSHES DOWN ON A SPECIAL **ELASTIC** MUSCLE, WHILE A CATCH HOLDS IT DOWN, LIKE A TIGHT SPRING.

AS THE FLEA JUMPS, THE CATCH RELEASES AND THE MUSCLE SHOOTS THE FLEA HIGH IN THE AIR.

DAVID SUZUKI ASKS DID YOU KNOW...

...WHY YOUR HANDS GET STIFF CARRYING HEAVY SHOPPING BAGS?

WHEN YOU EXERCISE, YOUR MUSCLES USE OXYGEN TO TURN SUGAR IN YOUR BLOOD INTO **ENERGY.** DURING VERY HARD WORK, STUFF CALLED **LACTIC ACID** IS MADE ALONG WITH THE ENERGY.

WHEN LACTIC ACID BUILDS UP FASTER THAN IT CAN BE TAKEN AWAY, THE MUSCLES STIFFEN UP. IF YOU THEN RELAX, THE MUSCLES CAN CATCH UP AND GET LOOSER AGAIN.

DAVID SUZUKI ASKS DID YOU KNOW...

...WHY DEAD ANIMALS GET STIFF?

WHEN ANIMALS (OR PEOPLE) ARE ALIVE, THEY MAKE A CHEMICAL CALLED **ATP** THAT KEEPS EACH MUSCLE CELL FREE TO MOVE.

BUT WHEN THE ANIMAL DIES, NO MORE ATP IS MADE. ONE BY ONE, THE MUSCLE CELLS START TO FREEZE IN PLACE, UNTIL THE WHOLE BODY IS AS STIFF AS A BOARD.

DAVID SUZUKI ASKS DID YOU KNOW...

...WHY THERE ARE "INNIE" AND "OUTIE" BELLYBUTTONS?

WHILE INSIDE YOUR MOTHER, YOU BREATHED AND WERE FED THROUGH AN UMBILICAL CORD. AFTER BIRTH, THE CORD WAS USELESS, AND WAS CUT OFF.

THE CORD STUB FELL OFF, LEAVING A SCAR: YOUR BELLYBUTTON. WHETHER YOU'RE AN INNIE OR AN OUTIE JUST DEPENDS ON HOW YOUR SCAR HEALED.

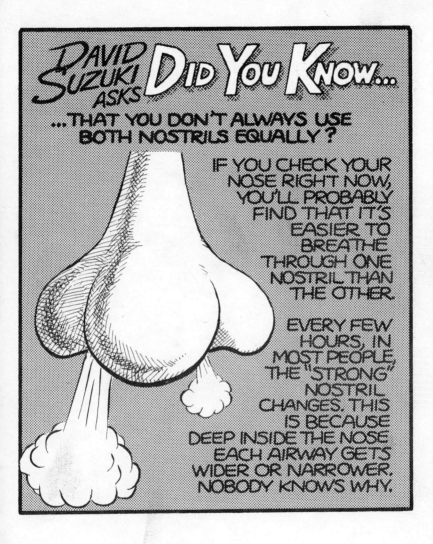

DAVID SUZUKI ASKS DID YOU KNOW...

...HOW SNAKES USE THEIR TONGUES TO SMELL?

WHEN A SNAKE'S TONGUE FLICKS OUT, BITS OF SCENTS CATCH ONTO IT.

WHEN THE TONGUE GOES BACK INTO THE MOUTH, IT TOUCHES AN ORGAN (CALLED JACOBSON'S ORGAN) THAT IS VERY SENSITIVE TO SCENTS. A SNAKE'S NOSTRILS ALSO LEAD TO THIS ORGAN.

BUT SNAKES' TONGUES DON'T HAVE TASTE BUDS, SO SNAKES CAN'T TASTE!

DAVID SUZUKI ASKS DID YOU KNOW...

...WHY DOGS STICK THEIR HEADS OUT OF CAR WINDOWS?

A DOG HAS AN AMAZING SENSE OF SMELL. BY STICKING ITS HEAD OUT OF A MOVING CAR'S WINDOW, A DOG CAN SMELL MANY SCENTS RUSHING BY.

ALL THESE SMELLS, ALONG WITH THE SIGHTS WHIZZING PAST, ARE VERY STIMULATING TO A DOG--PROBABLY LIKE AN EXCITING LIGHT SHOW IS TO US.

DAVID SUZUKI ASKS DID YOU KNOW...

...WHY ADULTS' ARMPITS SMELL?

THERE ARE TWO TYPES OF SWEAT. EVERYONE GETS ONE KIND ALL OVER THEIR BODIES; IT'S MADE MOSTLY OF WATER AND SALT, AND DOESN'T SMELL.

ONLY TEENAGERS AND ADULTS HAVE THE SECOND, ARMPIT KIND OF SWEAT. THIS SWEAT CONTAINS **FATS** WHICH ARMPIT BACTERIA LOVE TO EAT. AS THEY EAT, THEY MULTIPLY AND GIVE OFF STINKY CHEMICALS.

DAVID SUZUKI ASKS DID YOU KNOW...

...IF DOGS SWEAT?

A FEW ANIMALS (LIKE HORSES, APES, AND PEOPLE) SWEAT TO COOL DOWN. MOST OTHER MAMMALS DON'T HAVE MANY **SWEAT GLANDS**, SO THEY HAVE TO KEEP COOL OTHER WAYS.

DOGS CAN ONLY SWEAT A LITTLE (FROM THEIR PAWS), SO THEY GET RID OF EXTRA HEAT BY STICKING OUT THEIR WET TONGUES AND PANTING.

PUFF PUFF

BIRDS HAVE NO SWEAT GLANDS -- SO THEY PANT TO COOL OFF, TOO.

...HOW HIPPOS SUNBATHE?

HIPPOS DON'T HAVE **SWEAT GLANDS** IN THEIR SKIN, SO THEY HAVE TO SOAK IN WATER TO KEEP COOL. BUT THEY DO HAVE SKIN GLANDS THAT MAKE A THICK, PINKISH-RED GOOP.

THIS GOOP OOZES OVER ITS SKIN AND DRIES LIKE A VARNISH. THE PINK COATING HELPS TO PROTECT THE HIPPO FROM SUNBURN.

DAVID SUZUKI IS A SCIENCE BROADCASTER, WRITER, ENVIRONMENTALIST AND NOTED "INNIE."

LAURA MIYE SUZUKI IS A WRITER/ CARTOONIST, WHO EATS HER ICE CREAM TOO SLOWLY TO GET A HEADACHE. SHE IS AN "INNIE."

PETER COOK IS A CARTOONIST/WRITER WHO HAS A LARGE COLLECTION OF ALLERGIES THAT KEEP HIM COMPANY SIX MONTHS OF THE YEAR. SORRY, HE IS ALSO AN "INNIE."